Hazen Memorial Library
3 Keady Way
Shirley, MA 01464
978.425.2620

Glorious
Geometry

Lisa Arias

rourkeeducationalmedia.com

Before Reading:

Building Academic Vocabulary and Background Knowledge

Before reading a book, it is important to tap into what your child or students already know about the topic. This will help them develop their vocabulary, increase their reading comprehension, and make connections across the curriculum.

1.   *Look at the cover of the book. What will this book be about?*
2.   *What do you already know about the topic?*
3.   *Let's study the Table of Contents. What will you learn about in the book's chapters?*
4.   *What would you like to learn about this topic? Do you think you might learn about it from this book? Why or why not?*
5.   *Use a reading journal to write about your knowledge of this topic. Record what you already know about the topic and what you hope to learn about the topic.*
6.   *Read the book.*
7.   *In your reading journal, record what you learned about the topic and your response to the book.*
8.   *After reading the book complete the activities below.*

Content Area Vocabulary
Read the list. What do these words mean?

acute

angles

endpoint

intersect

line

line of symmetry

line segment

obtuse

parallel lines

perpendicular

protractor

ray

right angle

vertex

After Reading:

Comprehension and Extension Activity

After reading the book, work on the following questions with your child or students in order to check their level of reading comprehension and content mastery.

1.   *Explain why a straight line measures 180 degrees. (Asking questions)*
2.   *What does a protractor measure? (Summarize)*
3.   *Where do you see parallel lines in your community? (Text to self connection)*
4.   *What is the difference between an acute and an obtuse triangle? (Summarize)*
5.   *Are you symmetrical? Explain. (Text to self connection)*

Extension Activity

Using a ruler, pencil, and sheet a paper you can create tessellation math art! Starting in the middle of your paper draw a set of parallel lines going up, to the right, to the left, or going down. Wherever you choose to draw them you must draw a matching set in the opposite direction. Remember that parallel lines don't touch. This means you can have straight lines or curvy lines just as long as they don't touch. Continue drawing parallel lines until you have covered your paper with parallel line patterns. Once you are finished color in your creation!

Table of Contents

Lines, Angles, and Shapes

In everything you see you can spot lines, **angles**, and shapes. Yes, sirree.

Each and every point allows you to see
the exact location of things and where they should be.

● Point

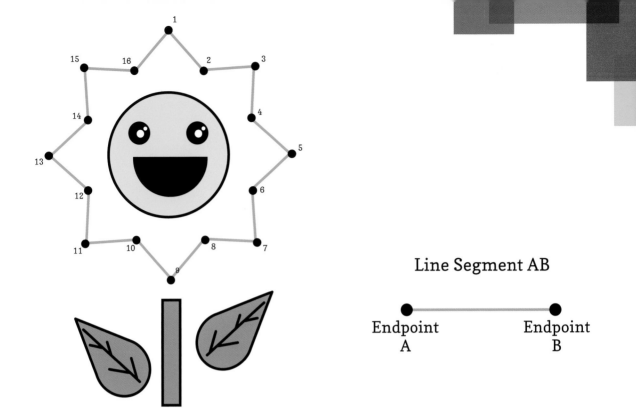

Line Segment AB

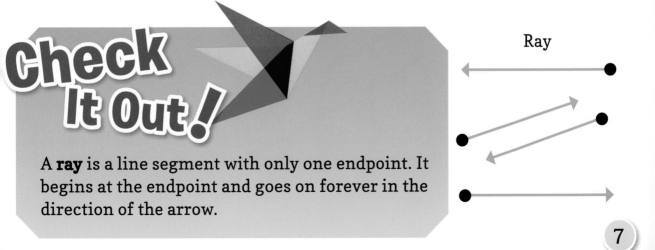

Endpoint
A

Endpoint
B

Drawing a **line segment** is easy to do,
just simply connect a point or two.

Once the points are connected,
they become the endpoints for the **line** selected.

Line segments are named by the endpoints they contain.

Check It Out!

Ray

A **ray** is a line segment with only one endpoint. It begins at the endpoint and goes on forever in the direction of the arrow.

Parallel Lines

Parallel lines run in the same direction.
They will never touch.

The symbol | | shows that two lines are parallel.
Thank you very much.

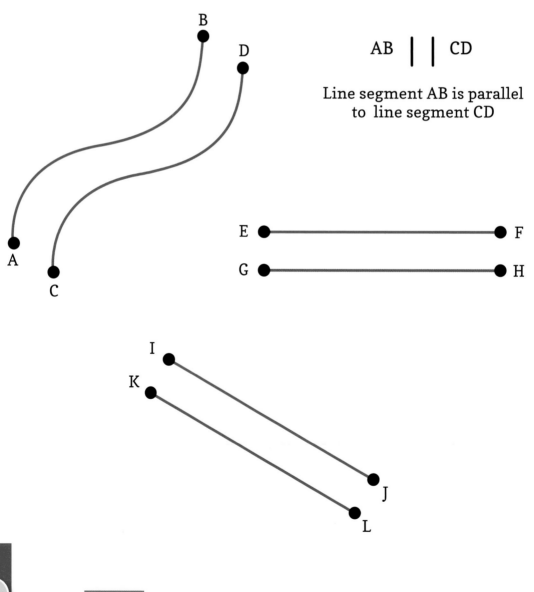

AB | | CD

Line segment AB is parallel
to line segment CD

Find the parallel lines.

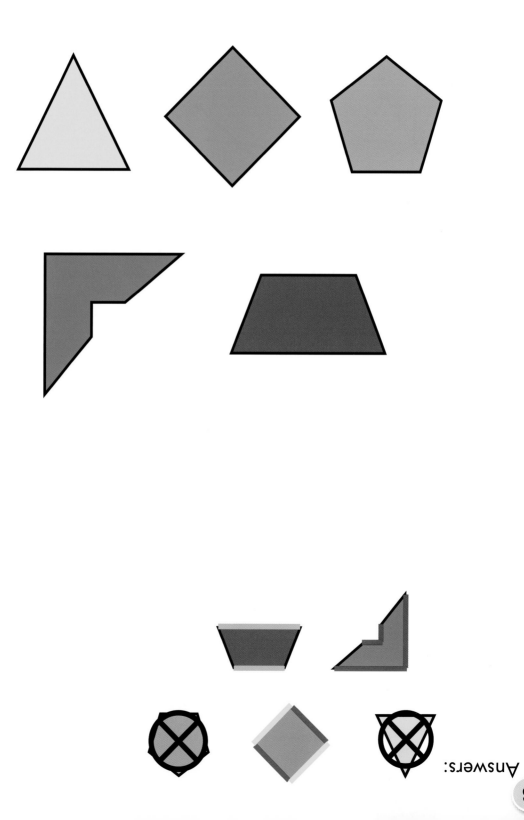

Crossing Lines

Angles form when lines or rays **intersect** at an **endpoint** called a **vertex**.

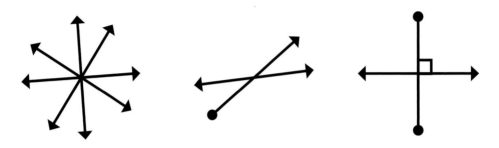

Angles are measured in degrees.
The degree symbol ° gives the amount you can see.

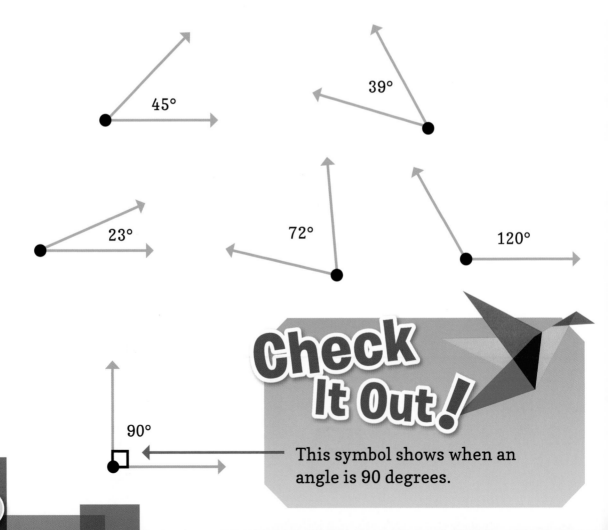

45°

39°

23°

72°

120°

90°

Check It Out!

This symbol shows when an angle is 90 degrees.

Perpendicular lines form 90 degree angles.

The perpendicular symbol ⊥ means you have nothing to untangle.

Find the perpendicular lines inside each shape.

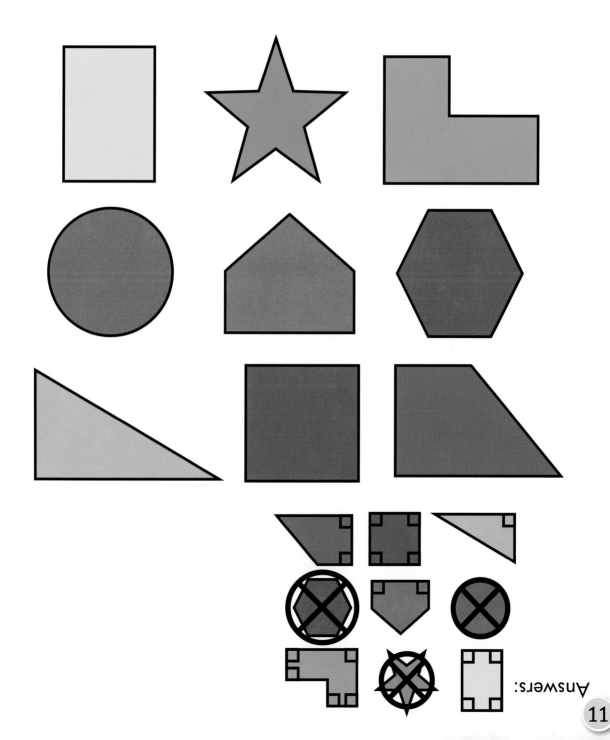

11

Naming Angles

Using letters and the angle symbol ∠ are helpful tools, to label and describe angles when you're in school.

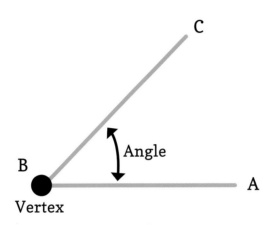

There are many ways to describe angles. To cite the angle on this page you can write:

∠CBA

or

∠ABC

or

∠B

Angles in circles can be related quite easily
as long as the equal parts add up to 360.

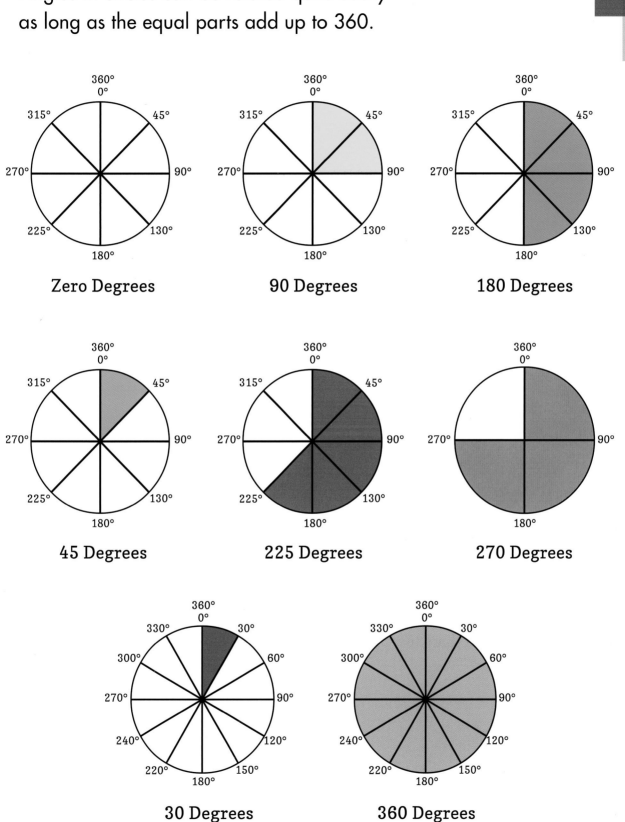

Zero Degrees

90 Degrees

180 Degrees

45 Degrees

225 Degrees

270 Degrees

30 Degrees

360 Degrees

Angles can also be described by their measure.

No matter the degree, every angle falls has a category.

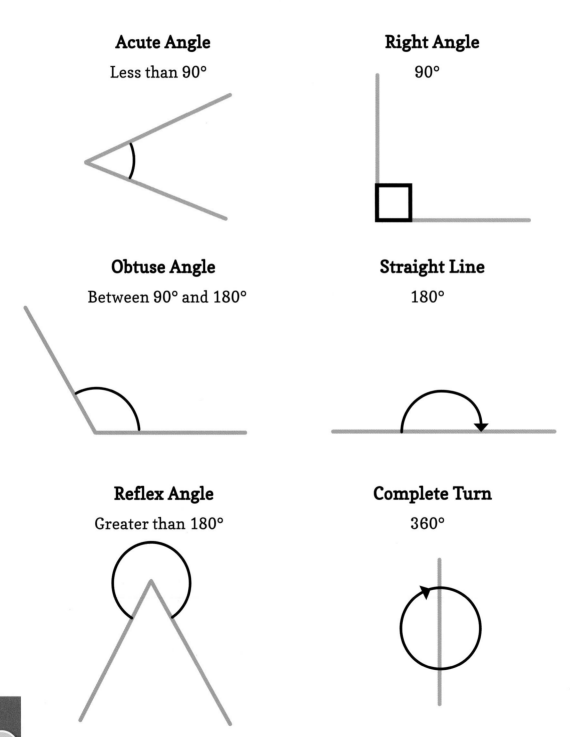

Acute Angle

Less than 90°

Right Angle

90°

Obtuse Angle

Between 90° and 180°

Straight Line

180°

Reflex Angle

Greater than 180°

Complete Turn

360°

Describe each angle as **acute**, right, or **obtuse**.

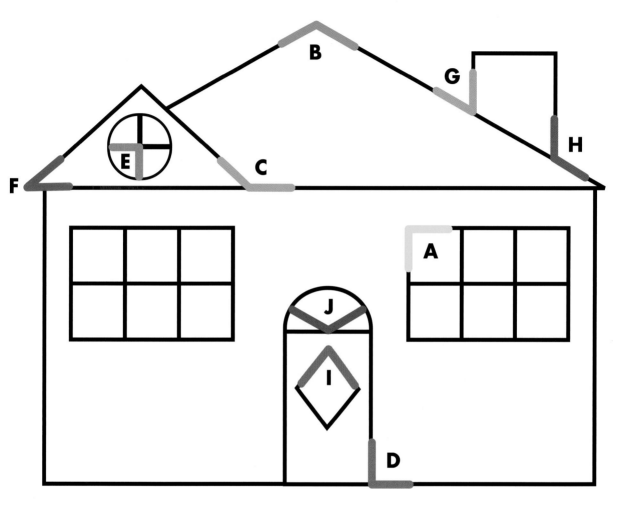

Find Unknown Angles

Finding the degree of a missing measure is a breeze
when you think about the missing measure's part in a known category.

90° – 70° = 20°

The missing angle and the known angle form a **right angle**. To find
the missing angle measure, subtract 70 degrees from 90 degrees.

180° – 40° = 140°

The missing angle and the known angle form a straight angle. To find
the missing angle measure, subtract 40 degrees from 180 degrees.

180° – 93° = 87°

The missing angle along with the two known angles form a straight
angle. To find the missing angle measure, subtract the known angles
from 180 degrees.

Find the missing angle measure.

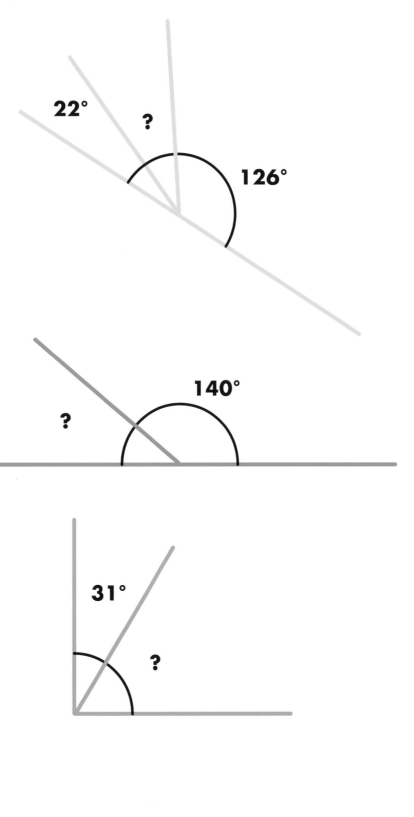

22°

?

126°

140°

?

31°

?

Measuring Angles

A **protractor** is a helpful tool
used to measure angles at home and at school.

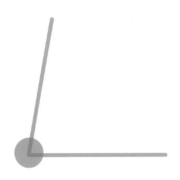

To measure an angle, begin by placing the center mark on the protractor
over the vertex of the angle you are measuring.

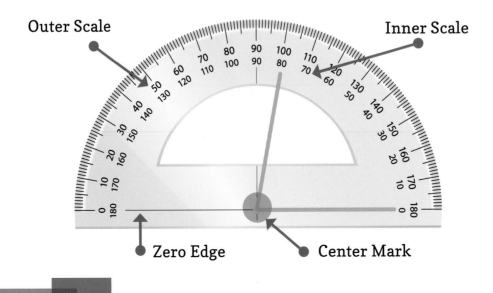

Outer Scale   Inner Scale

Zero Edge   Center Mark

Next, align the zero edge on the protractor with the line of the angle you are measuring.

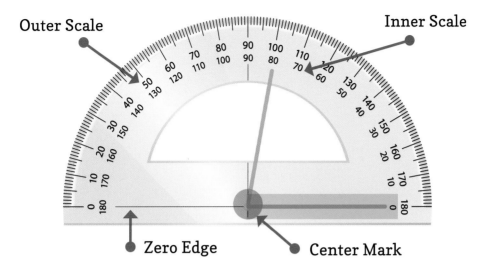

To find the correct measure, always use the scale that begins with zero.

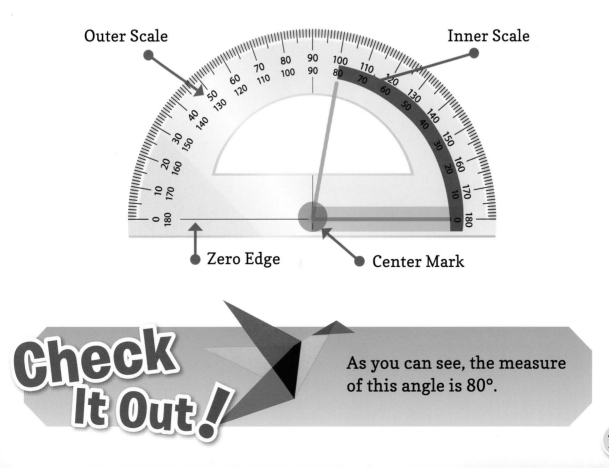

Check It Out!

As you can see, the measure of this angle is 80°.

Measure each angle.

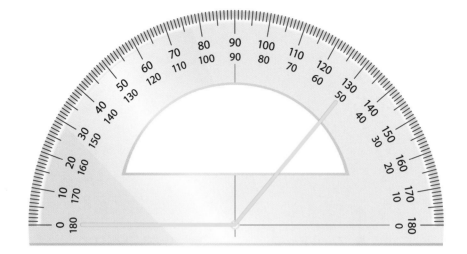

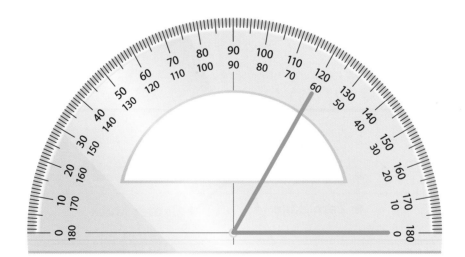

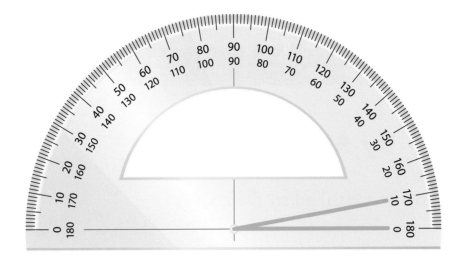

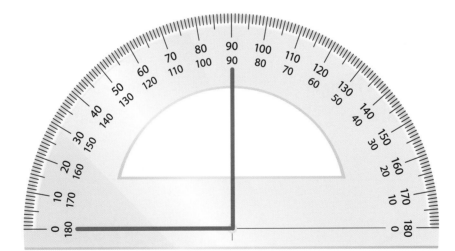

21

Classify by Side

Triangles can be classified by their sides.

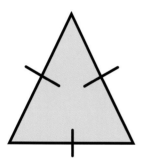

Equilateral Triangle

3 equal sides

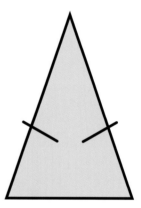

Isosceles Triangle

2 equal sides

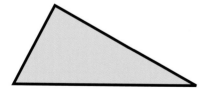

Scalene Triangle

no equal sides

Another name for equal is congruent. Lines are used to show that angles and sides are congruent.

22

Identify each triangle as equilateral, isosceles, or scalene.

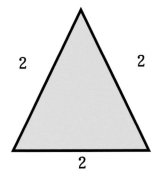

2   2

2

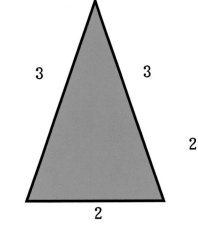

3   3

2

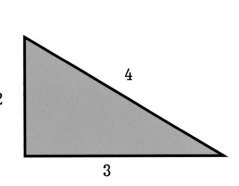

2   4

3

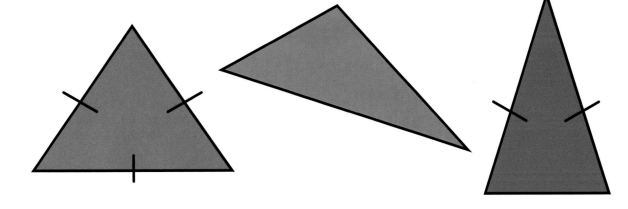

Classify by Angle

Triangles can also be classified by their angles.

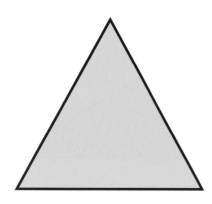

Acute Triangle

3 acute angles

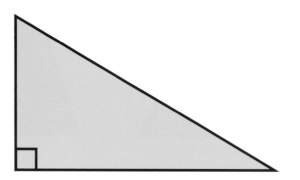

Right Triangle

1 right angle

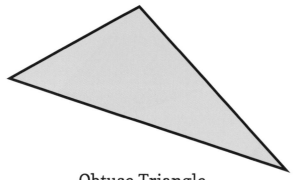

Obtuse Triangle

1 obtuse angle

The sum of the angles in a triangle equal 180 degrees.

Classify each triangle as acute, right, or obtuse.

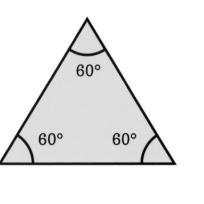

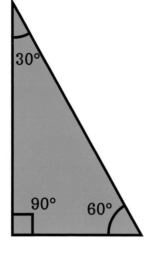

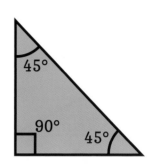

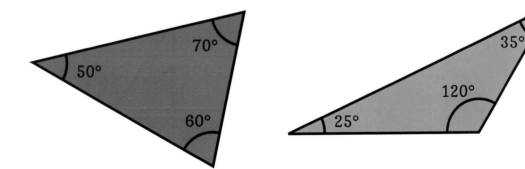

Answers:

Acute

Right

Right

Obtuse

Acute

25

Classify by Angle and Side

Now the time has arrived to classify triangles by their angle and side.

First classify the triangle by angle, then by side.

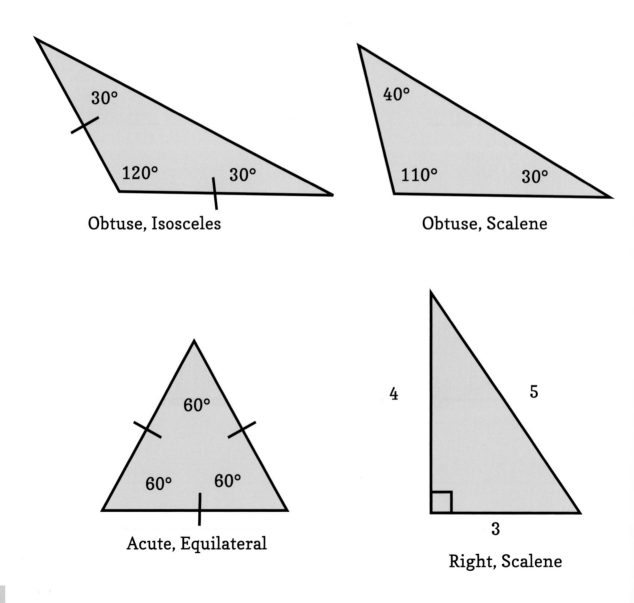

30°
120°   30°
Obtuse, Isosceles

40°
110°   30°
Obtuse, Scalene

60°
60°   60°
Acute, Equilateral

4   5
3
Right, Scalene

Classify each triangle by angle and side.

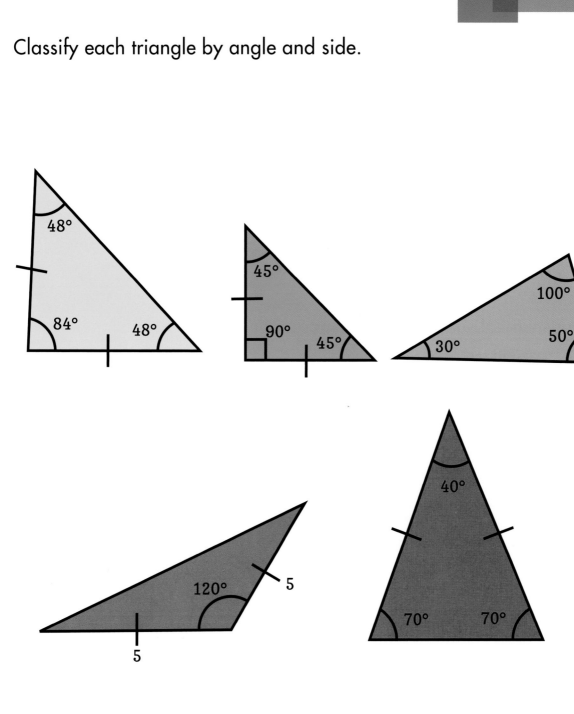

Symmetry

The symmetry of a shape is something you see
if you look at the opposite sides of a shape very carefully.

It is easy to do, imagine the shape folded in half.

If both sides are identical, then the shape is symmetrical.

A symmetrical shape can have more than one **line
of symmetry!**

Choose the shapes with the correct line or lines of symmetry shown.

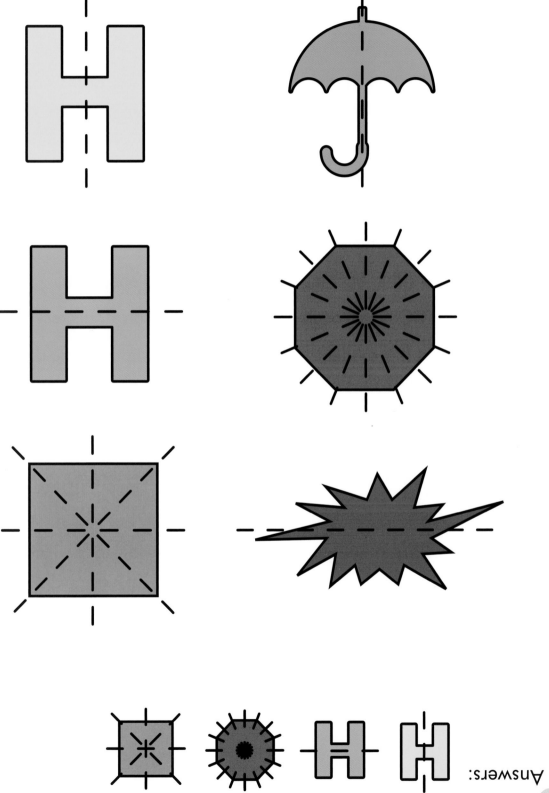

Glossary

acute: (uh-KYOOT): an angle measuring less than 90 degrees

angles (ANG-guhlz): lines or rays that intersect at an endpoint called a vertex

endpoint (END-POINT): the beginning point of a ray or the points found on each end of a line segment

intersect (in-tur-SEKTT): to cross over

line (LINE): infinite points continuing to infinity in both directions

line of symmetry (LINE uv SIM-uh-tree): an imaginary line that splits a shape into two identical parts

line segment (LINE SEG-muhnt): a line with two endpoints

obtuse (uhb-TOOSS): an angle measuring greater than 90 degrees

parallel lines (PA-ruh-lel LINES): lines that remain the same distance apart and will never intersect

perpendicular (pur-pehn-DIK-yoh-lur): intersecting lines that form 90 degree angles

protractor (proh-TRAK-tur): a tool used to measure angles

ray (RAY): a line segment with only one endpoint

right angle (RITE ANG-guhl): an angle measuring exactly 90 degrees

vertex (VUR-teks): a point where two or more rays or lines meet

Index

Websites to Visit

www.innovationslearning.co.uk/subjects/maths/activities/year6/angles/
    game.asp

www.mathplayground.com/measuringangles.html

www.oswego.org/ocsd-web/games/bananahunt/bhunt.html

About the Author

Lisa Arias is a math teacher who lives in Tampa, Florida with her husband and two children. Her out-of-the-box thinking and love for math guided her toward becoming an author. She enjoys playing board games and spending time with family and friends.

Meet The Author!
www.meetREMauthors.com

PHOTO CREDITS: Cover: © cienpies; Page 18: © tilo; all other illustrations © Tara Raymo

Edited by: Jill Sherman

Cover and Interior design by: Tara Raymo

Library of Congress PCN Data

Glorious Geometry: Lines, Angles and Shapes, Oh My! / Lisa Arias
(Got Math!)
ISBN 978-1-62717-713-9 (hard cover)
ISBN 978-1-62717-835-8 (soft cover)
ISBN 978-1-62717-948-5 (e-Book)
Library of Congress Control Number: 2014935590

Printed in the United States of America, North Mankato, Minnesota

Also Available as: